Leadership: Why Managers Fail?

10 Mistakes to Avoid When Managing People

A Practical Guidebook for Leaders and Managers

William L. Minix

A Practical Guidebook for Leaders and Managers

Managers, aspiring managers, and executives seeking to succeed at leading teams will benefit greatly from these insights. You don't have to fail as a manager, and knowing why others fail may rescue you from potential disaster. Learn from the mistakes others have made and avoid common pitfalls. This guidebook clearly identifies the challenges you face and provides simple instructions for managing and leading people.

AUTHOR	William L. Minix
CONTRIBUTORS	James D. Walton Vernita Harris
	Darryl Gresham Darien D. Davis
	Keith Osbourne Chuck Vivian
COPY EDITOR	Rochelle C. Guiton
PROOF READERS	Tracy Brown
	Patricia Pickles
	Omah Williams
	Shaunna Williams

Copyright © 2008 StarWise, Inc.

This book is copyrighted materials. All rights reserved. It is against the law to make copies of this material without getting specific written permission in advance from the author; this includes any reproduction, storage in a retrieval system, transmission, in any form or by any means, electronic, mechanical, photocopying, recording, or otherwise. Printed in the United States of America.

ISBN 978-1-7289249-1-5

"We Grow Leaders, Who Grow Business"

Dedication

This book is dedicated to God, who has ordered my steps throughout my life. To the memory of my wonderful parents, John and Maggie Minix, who provided the best childhood a boy could ask for, and the best advice a man could live by. And to my children, John Joseph (J.J.), and Mariana Minix whose presence warms my heart like none other.

Acknowledgements

Special thanks to:

My sisters and brothers, Zenobia, Teresa, Johnny, Joseph, and other family members for your enduring love and support.

Pastor Ralph Douglas West for your faithful leadership in guiding my spiritual growth, and for your encouragement.

Keith Osbourne for your dedication to teaching Sunday school and for sharing your knowledge and wisdom. Also to my classmates for your wonderful examples of how to commit to becoming better ambassadors for Christ.

Jim Walton and Darryl Gresham, for an entire career of mentoring and friendship.

Chuck Vivian for your willingness to share keen business insights, including your expert knowledge and counsel.

Pat Smith for encouraging me to package my knowledge and make it available to others. You have truly been an inspiration.

Andrew Morrison for providing me with the roadmap for this manuscript.

The thousands of people who have heard me speak and have inspired me to continue being an advocate for effective leadership.

Table of Contents

7	Introduction	
13	Mistake #1:	Promotion without Preparation
19	Mistake #2:	Expecting Immediate Respect and Trust
25	Mistake #3:	Making Decisions with No Input
29	Mistake #4:	Placing Job First, People Second
33	Mistake #5:	Accepting Credit, Assigning Blame
37	Mistake #6:	No Performance Management Plan
41	Mistake #7:	Limited Incentive Options
47	Mistake #8:	Thinking that Your Hands Are Tied
53	Mistake #9:	Not Having Systems of Accountability
59	Mistake #10:	No Barometers to Measure Success
63	Summary	
66	About the Author	

A Practical Guidebook for Leaders and Managers

Introduction

If you have people report directly to you, or aspire to someday, this guide will help you avoid the common pitfalls that keep managers and leaders from being successful. It will also help you with questions that most managers have, and are unable to answers. You will know what not to do as a manager and you will receive a roadmap for assuming responsibility of a team, influencing a culture, and developing loyal top performers.

From front line managers to executives, organizations seek to hire top talent as a means of driving business results. Much time and effort is devoted to this process, yet organizations struggle with the decision to develop and promote talent internally versus sourcing talent externally. We will discuss the importance of this decision and share insights regarding decision outcomes. The real questions are,

Leadership: Why Managers Fail

where do you fit in and what are you doing to develop yourself into a top contributor that continues to merit leadership consideration?

One of the first things you will notice in this guide is that the language, thoughts, and ideas are easy to understand and apply. I will model successful leadership traits, the first being "Keep it Simple". Everyone who reads this guide should take something away that they can do immediately to start the process of being a better leader. I will not insult your intelligence by telling you that you will become president of a firm in 90 days. However, I will share insights that could help you differentiate your leadership skills, and provide you with a competitive advantage in your leadership and managerial efforts.

Each chapter highlights a particular challenge that managers face in leading effectively. Following the characterization of each challenge are easy to remember bullet points noted as **Pitfalls, Pathways**, and **Direction**. *Pitfalls* are the things that you should avoid doing. They are counter-productive and may cause you to stumble and fail.

A Practical Guidebook for Leaders and Managers

Pathways are the things that you should invest in doing for yourself and others to enhance your likelihood of achieving success and significance. **Direction** gives you your roadmap. These tips are recommended for your use to enhance your leadership effectiveness. In order to change conditions, you must change your direction. The wisdom of each chapter is rolled up into these action items that you must apply to receive benefits from this guidebook.

Leadership: Why Managers Fail

Bottom - Line Up Front

Managers fail for lack of leadership. **Managers** control and direct processes, tasks, and expenditures. **Leaders** motivate, inspire, develop, and guide people. Understanding this distinction is paramount to understanding the rest of this manual.

All businesses exist to make money and many companies reward their top individual contributors by promoting them into the management ranks. Oftentimes individuals are even recruited into leadership roles after being tagged as high potential. There is nothing wrong with wanting to grow talent organically. Historically, the pitfall has been failure to prepare people for effective leadership.

A Practical Guidebook for Leaders and Managers

Managers control and direct processes, tasks, and expenditures.

Leaders motivate, inspire, develop, and guide people.

Leadership: Why Managers Fail

"Change is the only thing permanent in life; without it, innovation could never occur. Those who initiate change create great value and dictate outcomes rather than respond to them."

Bill Minix

A Practical Guidebook for Leaders and Managers

MISTAKE #1:

Promotion without Preparation

Leaders and managers contribute the greatest value to organizations seeking growth. Companies could protect and maintain valuable resources if they would invest in developing leadership internally to promote throughout the organization.

Promoting individual contributors to leadership roles without preparation is a formula for failure.

This would preserve organization knowledge and save lots of money. Without investing in leadership development, high performers are promoted without being prepared and they attempt to utilize the same skills as managers that made them successful as individual contributors. That is a formula for failure.

Leadership: Why Managers Fail

Hiring externally is a viable alternative to promoting internally. However, investment in leadership development is still warranted. New employees will still require training in leadership, management, and applicable company processes and common skills. Additionally, external hires will also benefit from assistance in adapting to a new culture, unless the employee has been brought in as a change agent. Even change agents often need guidance to assist them in effectively implementing new initiatives. Keep in mind that there are both pros and cons to external hiring. For example, a positive feature of hiring externally is that it will bring fresh ideas and more experience to the table. A possible downside to hiring externally is that it is demoralizing to your current employees who have worked hard and earned the right to be considered for jobs of increased responsibility.

Individuals who work for firms with no structured leadership development programs would be wise to seek out this training on their own.

Smart companies invest in the development of their people. Smart people invest in developing themselves.

A Practical Guidebook for Leaders and Managers

The investment will pay great dividends, as getting proper instructions on how to lead will help them avoid the common pitfalls that cause unprepared managers to derail.

Pitfalls:

• **Avoid:** Thinking you will succeed in management with skills used as an individual contributor

• **Avoid:** Over reliance on one particular strength; masking the need for new skill development

• **Avoid:** Being frustrated. There is always anxiety associated with change due to concerns of the unknown. Most feel incompetent and out of control because they are transitioning outside of their comfort zone.

Leadership: Why Managers Fail

Pathways:

- Learn new skills needed to lead and manage. Customize the learning to your environment. Spend the majority of your time building new skills in areas where you are naturally gifted and talented.

- Learn to leverage the talents of others to compliment both your strengths and limitations

- Prepare for leadership challenges before and during leadership assignments; leaders must continuously learn, grow, and change to sustain top performance

Direction - Your Action Items Are:

• Ask for leadership and managerial training in your organization or business. Make a personal investment if it is not otherwise available

• Commit to self-awareness training, such as Myers Briggs Type Indicator, and learn about individual differences. This is the foundation of effective communication, meaningful human interactions, and leadership

• Seek out mentors and thinking partners to serve as sounding boards. These individuals should be people with high levels of experience, success, and expertise. He or she must be willing to assist you. Self-monitoring is a mistake. Others provide objective feedback and different perspectives.

A Practical Guidebook for Leaders and Managers

- Align your passion, heart, and mind with things you choose to do and be great at it. Accepting new assignments will either polarize an area where you are strong, or offer critical skills needed to help prepare you for future roles of increased responsibility. Knowing that your new assignment is a means to an end will allow you to stay focused on achieving results and pursuing your passion.

Leadership: Why Managers Fail

"I have always challenged myself to walk with the best. When you start a new position, find the best and to walk with the best, you must gain their trust and respect. The best way to get it, is to outperform them!"

Jim Walton

A Practical Guidebook for Leaders and Managers

Mistake #2:
Expecting Immediate Respect and Trust

Many managers are surprised to learn that people don't bow down to titles or positions. Your place in an organization does not grant you sovereignty or absolute power because people don't arbitrarily place those in charge of them on a pedestal. Those who are deemed in the highest esteem get there by earning the respect and admiration of those they inspire.

To new managers' credit, they go into their new roles wanting to make a big positive impact in a relatively short period of time. The challenge they face is that people don't care how much you know until they know how much you care.

Respect and trust are earned by what you do; not by who you are, what you say, nor what you've done in the past.

Leadership: Why Managers Fail

To earn respect and trust, you must invest time getting to know your people personally and professionally. Don't go in "all guns blazing" looking to make changes immediately.

Find out from their perspective:

- What was family life like growing up?
- Find out if there are any big personal plans on the horizon.
- What motivates them?
- How do they like to be coached?
- What are their career goals and aspirations?
- How have they performed historically?
- How do they view success and what success impact are they planning to make?
- And finally, create opportunities for them to share anything they would like for you to know.

A Practical Guidebook for Leaders and Managers

Guard sacred the conversations you have and use information only for the purpose of building customized development plans to help grow your people. This lays the foundation for the differentiated conversations to come and for distinguishing you from the managers before you who only used confidential information to get things done. Follow up on commitments, and personalize incentives when possible. Your attitude towards each individual will set the tone and build mutual respect and trust.

Pitfalls:

- **Avoid:** Being power struck or demanding respect

- **Avoid:** Being a know-it-all or condescending

- **Avoid:** Asking people to trust you

Trust is hard to gain, and easily loss. Protect confidential information.

Leadership: Why Managers Fail

Pathways:

- Encourage input from others and earn respect by modeling sound judgment and good guidance

- Be mutually respectful and value insights from others

- Earn trust and respect through your actions. Ask people to trust in the vision or process; not in you

Direction – Your Action Items Are:

- Transition with a predecessor if possible or be introduced to your team
- Have 1-on-1's with all of your staff. Use the information on page 18 to guide your discussion
- Learn how they like to be coached and led. Plan accordingly

A Practical Guidebook for Leaders and Managers

Guard sacred the confidential conversations entrusted to you.

Earn respect by what you do. Model the success you want to see in others.

Leadership: Why Managers Fail

"Most discussions of decision making assumes that only senior executives make decisions or that only senior executives' decisions matter. This is a dangerous mistake."

Peter Drucker

"Plans fail for lack of counsel, but with many advisers they succeed."

Prov. 15:22(NIV)

A Practical Guidebook for Leaders and Managers

Mistake #3:
Making Decisions with No Input

Everyone wants to be heard, and people are more willing to believe what they say, than what you say. Also, two or more heads are better than one and having multiple perspectives weigh in will make for better decision making. You grow exponentially as a leader when you begin to value the wealth associated with information gathering from those closest to the problem. Keeping this in mind, don't make the mistake of thinking that you must have all the answers.

Even when you know the answer, be more apt to ask questions rather than make statements to allow for dialogue. This will help you build and encourage open communication with your people, and assess mutual understanding.

People want to have a voice. YOU MUST LISTEN.

Leadership: Why Managers Fail

People will feel better about your conversations because you are speaking with them and not at them.

Otherwise, be prepared for lots of cold blank stares and one-line canned responses. You know definitively that you have failed to lead your people when they stop bringing you their problems. Your goal is to coach your people to communicate good and bad information with the same ease. Superimposing your superior decision making into every conversation is a sure way to discourage meaningful dialogue.

Pitfalls:

Communication will decay overtime if you fail to listen. Don't get stuck with your own ideas

- **Avoid:** Discouraging or disregarding input from others
- **Avoid:** Playing favorites and limiting input to a select few
- **Avoid:** Establishing silos and barriers. Do not put up walls that obstruct communication inside or outside of your department.

A Practical Guidebook for Leaders and Managers

Pathways:

- Encourage open discussion about vision, goals, and objectives
- Involve as many people and ideas as possible
- Share information freely

Direction – Your Action Items Are:

- Agree on vision, and discuss past-current-future
- Involve your team in strategy meetings
- Quick team votes are often appropriate

Leadership: Why Managers Fail

"The key to leadership is simply being on the front line with your people. And don't lead from behind a desk."
Darryl Gresham

"I suppose leadership at one time meant muscles; but today it means getting along with people."
Mohandas Gandhi

"Without people there is no company; only empty assets with no engine to succeed."
Chuck Vivian

A Practical Guidebook for Leaders and Managers

Mistake #4:
Placing Job First, People Second

Time and time again managers struggle with this concept. They believe that attempts to motivate and persuade people to want to exceed expectations is "baby sitting" them. This is characteristic of those who have impersonal attitudes towards people. The focus here is on completing whatever tasks have been assigned or driving towards a particular goal or objective.

People are just a means for getting work done. The outcome of this approach is a demoralized workforce that feels overworked, undervalued, and underappreciated. Some success may be derived from this approach; however, this method will not sustain

> ***People were not made to rule over other people; we were made to work together.***

Leadership: Why Managers Fail

high performance levels and it will lead to high dissatisfaction, high turnover, low morale, and low levels of trust and loyalty. Whenever people attempt to rule or control other people, the only thing that can result is oppression.

People will run through walls for you when they discern that you are genuinely concerned for their well-being.

Put people first. It's not cliché when I say your people are your most important and most appreciable assets. Vision, mission, strategy, goals, and objectives are all important, and you cannot accomplish any of them without people. Invest the time to get to know your people professionally and personally. Understand what's important to each individual in your organization from their perspective. Your genuineness in this regard will convey your concern for your people's well-being. Apply this concept in your daily interactions and you distinguish your ability to build loyalty, trust, and adoration for your leadership effectiveness.

A Practical Guidebook for Leaders and Managers

Pitfalls:

- **Avoid:** Being task oriented
- **Avoid:** Focusing too much on processes, and not enough on results
- **Avoid:** Being driven by "To Do Lists"

Pathways:

- Let your people know you genuinely care about their well being
- You convey interest in their development and success
- Use each individual's personal vision for success to steer their actions

Direction – Your Action Items Are:

- Communicate your desire to see your people achieve the success they envision for themselves
- Celebrate success; professionally and personally
- Ask your team members how they are performing against their personal vision for success and how you can serve as a resource to them.

Leadership: Why Managers Fail

"The leaders who work most effectively, it seems to me, never say 'I.' And that's not because they have trained themselves not to say 'I.' They don't think 'I.' They think 'we;' they think 'team.' They understand their job is to make the team function. They accept responsibility and don't sidestep it, but 'we' gets the credit. This is what creates trust, what enables you to get the task done."

Peter Drucker

A Practical Guidebook for Leaders and Managers

Mistake #5:
Accepting Credit, Assigning Blame

One of the fastest ways to lose credibility is by never accepting ownership when things go wrong. By nature, managers who are process-driven seek to shun responsibility when problems arise. Yet they are more than willing to shoulder praise provided by leaders, while not acknowledging the efforts and contributions of their people. This flaw in the character of managers is often referred to as CYA ("Cover Your Assets"). It suggests that Managers should seek the appearance of being near perfect, and less prone to mistakes. The quest to achieve this perceptual status gives birth to the "blame game".

Give credit to your people when things go well, accept responsibility when things go wrong.

Leadership: Why Managers Fail

Pitfalls:

- **Avoid:** Taking all the credit for work, achievement and success
- **Avoid:** Passing the buck when things go wrong
- **Avoid:** Exposing people when problems occur

Pathways:

- Give credit to others for work achievement
- Accept responsibility when things go wrong
- Focus on problem resolution, and not on assigning blame

Direction – Your Action Items Are:

- Routinely communicate the role others play in achieving organizational success. Highlight their contributions, let others mention yours.
- State "I am ultimately responsible for all matters". If your people are not performing, it's your job to develop them to the point where they can perform.
- Look for the root cause of the problems. Agree on the best resolutions and how to achieve desired results in the future. Communicate corrective actions so that all may benefit from the lessons learned.

A Practical Guidebook for Leaders and Managers

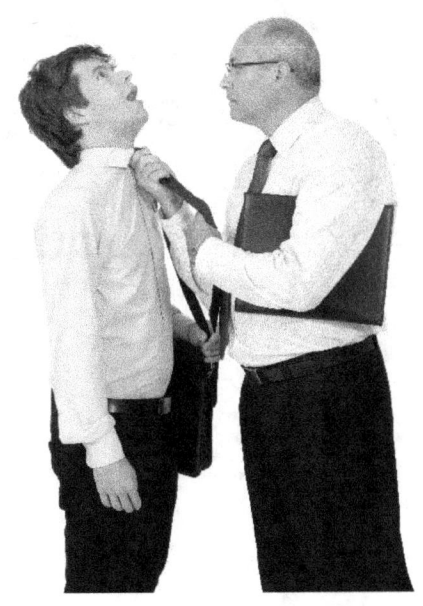

Focus on problem resolution, not on assigning blame.

Leadership: Why Managers Fail

"Planning is bringing the future into the present so that you can do something about it now."

Unknown

A Practical Guidebook for Leaders and Managers

Mistake #6:
No Performance Management Plan

Don't make the mistake of thinking you are too busy to develop performance plans jointly with each of the people you are responsible for. Taking the time to construct a plan to help your people develop is among the most valuable activities that you will perform. Eighty percent of success comes from having a well-defined plan and there is a direct correlation between developing your people and sustaining business growth. Often times, managers prioritize this activity very low, and in fact, most will not do it at all unless it is mandated by their employers. Even the mandates are ineffective as the performance management activity becomes a paper drill to managers who fail

Creating and sustaining top performance is directly correlated with your ability to develop your people.

Leadership: Why Managers Fail

to grasp its significance. Your people are perceptive, and whether spoken or not, they view a lack of collaborative career planning as a sign of manager and organization indifference.

People don't care how much you know until they know how much you care. A performance management plan is too important not to invest the time. Regarding the team you will lead, get to know what each of your personnel aspire to do with their career and commit to helping them to be successful. Study self-awareness, individual differences, and leadership principles to assist you in your preparation.

People don't care how much you know, until they know how much you care.

A Practical Guidebook for Leaders and Managers

Pitfalls:

- **Avoid:** Not having the knowledge and skills needed to develop people
- **Avoid:** Underestimating the impact of developing your people
- **Avoid:** Diminishing support, loyalty, and trust

Pathways:

- Understand the development process
- Implement growth plans, and demonstrate your genuine concern for others
- Involve your people in performance planning, encourage continuous improvement, and create an environment conducive to learning from mistakes

Direction – Your Action Items Are:

- Create a customized development plan with all of your people
- Oversee their growth and development; help build new knowledge, skills, and leadership attributes
- Orchestrate ways for new learning to be used. Acknowledge and reinforce successful use of newly acquired skills.

" The dogmas of the quiet past are inadequate to the stormy present. The occasion is piled high with difficulty, and we must rise with the occasion. As our case is new, so we must think anew and act anew."

Abraham Lincoln

A Practical Guidebook for Leaders and Managers

Mistake #7:
Limited Incentive Options

Don't make the mistake of being limited in the ways you choose to incentivize your teams. There are many sources of motivation that may be used to encourage behavior. Most managers view life as a dichotomous "either - or". The tendency is to turn to the "stick" or the "carrot". The choice is limited to either placing fear in their people with financial incentive programs. Never use fear and smear as a means of motivation. This method may achieve some short-term results, but it will never yield long term loyalty and support. In the end, fear and smear does more damage than good. Financial incentives are okay and useful in placing focus on strategic objectives. However, if leaders are not careful, they may overuse money incentives and distract from its effectiveness long term.

Leadership: Why Managers Fail

Only throw money at strategic initiatives that have a time sensitivity that clearly supports the investment.

A financial incentive plan is only one source of motivation and believe it or not; it does not appeal to all people. Some people are not motivated by money. A few other sources of motivation include meaningful work, job stability, environment, work-life balance, sense of family, teamwork, goal accomplishment, recognition, rewards, and paid time off of work. Your role as a leader is to uncover the source of motivation for each member on your team and creatively appeal to the individual. Exploring options for incentives with your team is a good way to involve them and motivate them. Even if you are unable to implement their ideas, the value of your efforts to appease their source of motivation will yield higher levels of commitment and support.

Money does not motivate everyone.

All people are unique. Learn what motivates each individual you lead.

A Practical Guidebook for Leaders and Managers

Pitfalls:

- **Avoid:** Fear and Smear tactics; Negative stimulus will only produce boomerangs that will be harmful long-term

- **Avoid:** Limiting your options; Be open to creative ideas

- **Avoid:** Redundancy; Routine incentive programs may lose their appeal

Pathways:

- Find unique and creative ways to incentivize your people

- Explore customized incentive options based on the uniqueness of your team

- Involve your people in exploring options; benefit from their insights

Leadership: Why Managers Fail

Direction – Your Action Items Are:

- Ask your people what motivates them; this is the best way to learn

- Agree on customized incentive plans. Sell your ideas to decision- makers.

- Link incentives directly to your team's source of motivation. You can communicate multiple benefits from one plan. Make your conversations personal.

A Practical Guidebook for Leaders and Managers

FAMILY　　　　　　**MONEY**

People have different sources of motivation. Find out what motivates each of your people.

VACATION　　　　　　**TEAMWORK**

Other Sources:

REWARDS, RECOGNITION, WORK-LIFE BALANCE, ENVIRONMENT, JOB SECURITY ...

> "When you discover your mission, you will feel its demand. It will fill you with enthusiasm and a burning desire to get to work on it."
>
> W. Clement Stone

> "You have all the resources you need to be successful. It's up to you to: Access them with creativity; Use them with purpose; and have faith you will succeed."
>
> Dan Duster

A Practical Guidebook for Leaders and Managers

Mistake #8:

Thinking that Your Hands are Tied

You are not helpless and you exist to make a difference. Don't wait on others to tell you your every move. Organizations are full of followers sitting in leadership roles and most are just occupying seats that belong to someone else. Leaders are supposed to make a difference and you must develop courage to be effective. Dare to be proactive; dare to promote new ideas and concepts; and dare to support your people.

The only thing keeping you from being powerful is you.

Leadership: Why Managers Fail

Your current level in the organization does not matter. Organizations will cater to good ideas regardless of their source of origin. The mere fact that you can imagine better possibilities speaks to your visionary capabilities. Simply thinking of ways to continuously improve business practices and processes will place you in the top 20 percent of your peer group. Yes, managers will attack you for wanting to make a difference. Their job is to protect status quo which is an organizational killer. Your role as a leader is to continuously reinvent yourself and your organization to keep pace with change. Sometimes that means being ahead of it, sometimes aligned, and sometimes deciding to lag behind it. However, leaders always think through options and decide ahead of time. Right now, think of the things that your organization should start, alter, or stop doing. Think through the best way to communicate one or two of your recommendations and act on them within 72 hours of reading this text.

You can lead from anywhere in the organization.

A Practical Guidebook for Leaders and Managers

Pitfalls:

- **Avoid:** Feeling powerless; Don't wait for others to tell you your

    every move

- **Avoid:** Thinking you must be in a higher position to lead
- **Avoid:** Feeling sunk if the boss is a bad leader

Pathways:

- Empower yourself by instituting new and creative ways to improve performance
- Know that leaders are required at all levels. You can influence from where you are.
- Leading means making your boss look good. Use your effectiveness to cover his/her flaws. This may mean acting first and asking for forgiveness later.

Leadership: Why Managers Fail

Direction – Your Action Items Are:

- Enroll in leadership training. Understand what it means to lead so that you can practice developing good skills.
- Start transforming immediately. It may be tough because society conditions us to believe that others are leaders. Everyone who touches this text was born to lead. You have been equipped by the creator with natural gifts and talents. Discover what they are and start developing them right away.
- Fix the little things first. Build empowerment.
- Prioritize change with vision, mission, and objectives

```
"First be a leader;

followers will come."
```

Chuck Vivian

A Practical Guidebook for Leaders and Managers

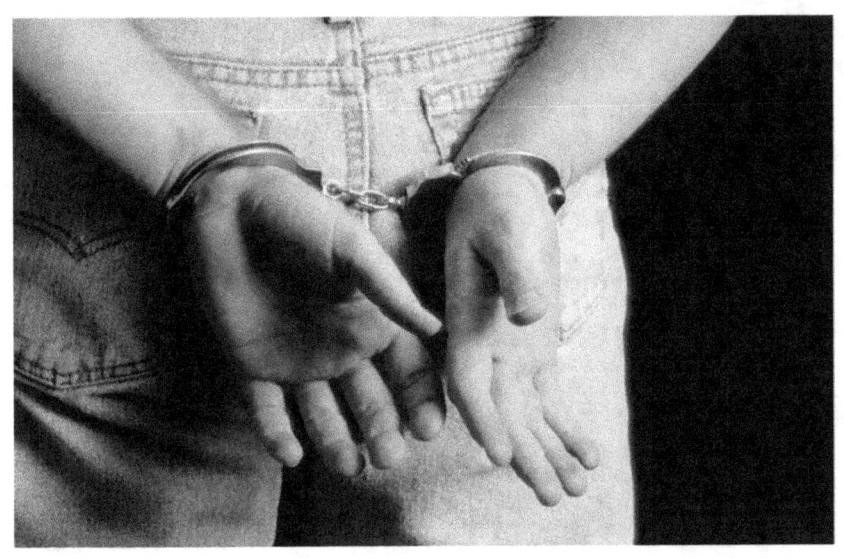

You are not powerless

and

you have the liberty

to do something great.

"Great things happen when leaders show up, and it doesn't happen by chance. It happens because ordinary people demonstrate the ability to achieve extraordinary results routinely."

Bill Minix

A Practical Guidebook for Leaders and Managers

Mistake #9:
Not Having Systems of Accountability

It matters not how well you are able to motivate and inspire people, if you don't have standards and measures in place to govern activities and behaviors, you will fail. What are systems of accountability? I am glad you asked. Systems of accountability are the published expectations that a leader uses to guide and direct team members who agree to ownership of the published responsibilities. The expectations explicitly address performance and behavior standards including but not limited to planning, people interactions, administration, and reporting activities.

Sustained success occurs when everyone understands and appreciates the valuable role they play.

Leadership: Why Managers Fail

Examples of systems of accountability may include:

1. Weekly Activity Plan & Report – A forward look at activities planned to drive results in the coming week, and to report success from the previous week. The proactive plan provides the strategy for the next action steps required, including resources needed to be successful.

2. Monthly Highlights – Captures significant accomplishments for the month for high-level reporting. Also highlights activity in the marketplace which may affect business, such as competitive activity, price, quality, politics, and others.

3. Monthly Updates – 30 minutes to an hour of dedicated time devoted to each of your employees to resolve their challenges and issues.

A Practical Guidebook for Leaders and Managers

This is their time and personal access to you. Note a saying from General Colin Powell, Chairman (Ret), Joint Chiefs of Staff and Former U.S. Secretary of State, "The day soldiers stop bringing you their problems is the day you have stopped leading them". Substitute the word "people" for "soldiers" and the same premise holds true in the public and private sectors. There is both an art and a science to effective leadership and putting systems of accountability in place ties them both together.

Pitfalls:

- **Avoid:** Not having a plan to drive business success
- **Avoid:** Lacking the courage to have tough conversations and hold people accountable
- **Avoid:** Not having metrics in place to track key success drivers

Leadership: Why Managers Fail

Pathways:

- Have an activity-based action plan and publish details governing how the plan will be incorporated and administered

- Assign roles, responsibilities, and activities that are clearly stated and well-understood

- Coach: be persistent at reinforcing the right activities and behaviors

-

Direction – Your Action Items Are:

- Develop and communicate an action plan for leading

- Publish roles and coaching engagements

- Routinely write assessments of observed behavior and set expectations for future growth

A Practical Guidebook for Leaders and Managers

Clearly communicate your vision and success plan.

Communicate roles and responsibilities and hold people accountable.

Provide written performance assessments routinely; link to performance expectations.

Leadership: Why Managers Fail

"80% of success comes from having a well-defined plan. Without barometers to measure critical success factors, the likelihood of succeeding is nil and the prognosis of failure is great."

Bill Minix

Mistake #10:
No Barometers to Measure Success

If you can't measure it you can't control it. You will inevitably find a way to track key success factors for any activity that you are serious about. Quantification gives you a good objective way of monitoring performance and predicting successes or failures. Success however, is not always measured in numbers. It is up to you as a leader to discern which activities to measure.

Don't measure for the sake of measuring. If the data you collect is not useful in growing business, predicting success or failure, enhancing your odds of achieving success, or making financial decisions, then don't do it.

Highly effective leaders identify the right activities to monitor and track.

In contrast, if there is a direct correlation between data you collect and an increase or decrease in sales, enrollment, productivity or efficiency then measure it periodically.

Remember this, you inspire people, and manage numbers. Managers fail often by making the mistake of using numbers to manage people. The numbers are not the most important thing, the people are. Keep this in perspective when receiving, sharing, or distributing data. The details are always in the conversation and it is not what the data suggests, but rather the message you convey that matters choose to be positive, inspire and encourage, or be negative, demoralize and deflate. *Inspire People, and Manage Numbers*

Good people with the right motivation can always turn around bad numbers. People who are made to feel inept, are unlikely to become force multipliers. Talk about numbers as it relates to the future, not the past. Focus on where the numbers are headed, verses where they are and be honest and optimistic. You have the power to will success in your people. Don't just be a thermometer like most managers and take the temperature of your people. Be a thermostat and regulate the temperature. Your leadership can cause numbers to go up, and focusing your people on the right activities with supporting data will drive business results.

Pitfalls:

- **Avoid:** Failing to monitor and track key success factors
- **Avoid:** Managing people with numbers
- **Avoid:** Using numbers to beat people up about past performance

Pathways:

- Understand what your key business drivers are and monitor them periodically
- Communicate frequently with your personnel using supporting data. Focus on activities, motivation, and results; not numbers
- Provide vision for where the numbers are going and what must be done to get there

- Focus on the impact and implications of numbers, good and bad, in the future

Direction – Your Action Items Are:

- Develop a prioritized list of key business drivers. Understand the historical significance and verify accuracy.

  For example, if you sell capital equipment you can use numbers to predict success. On average in a highly competitive field, a representative may win 3 deals in 10. If this representative has a quota of 3 units per month they must work on a minimum of 10 qualified decisions each month. As a leader, you may wish to require 12 to 15 decisions be worked each month to assure success.

- Schedule 1-on-1's and team meetings. Focus on next steps, action items, and resource requirements.

- Publish updates on key metrics to stakeholders. Highlight successes and communicate planned increases or decreases.

- Share the trust, confidence, and belief that you have in your people's ability to achieve desired results.

- You must say it to convey it, and your spoken words of encouragement will stimulate their intrinsic desire to succeed.

Summary

My desire is to help you optimize your leadership potential, and equip you with a roadmap to help develop other leaders.

Companies, communities, and humanity will benefit from understanding effective leadership.

The advice offered in this text is intended to help you navigate successfully through the mine fields of leadership and management. The tips and techniques are based on lessons learned from my life's experiences and captured and shared for your benefit. They are the result of things that I have done both right and wrong, my observations of other leaders both good and bad, and persistent conscientious study of human behavior. My desire is that you may use this knowledge to avoid common mistakes, and make your path to success less troublesome. It is also intended to help those you are responsible for leading receive better guidance, direction, and development. Inevitably, both individuals and organizations should benefit from incorporating these principles into daily regiments. I have made it a personal mission to help grow leaders who grow organizations.

My company StarWise, Inc. was founded to help fill a void of leadership in the private and public sector.

I want to further advise you to test every principle belief in this text against a reference to ensure that it offers wise council. What should you use as a referee when you either disagree or you are uncertain about a principle I've shared? I am glad you asked. Imagine you are playing the board game Scrabble. When there is a word that you are uncertain of, and you wish to challenge its legitimacy you use a dictionary. The dictionary then becomes your reference point and your referee. In the dictionary you find both clarity and definition to satisfy your word conflict. Someone once asked me, "What is the best book that you ever read on leadership?" The question was posed to establish better understanding of a reference that I should use to establish my philosophical beliefs. Never having been asked that question before, I began to list several of my favorite leadership books including Dr. Myles Munroe's <u>The Spirit of Leadership</u>, <u>The Principles and Power of Vision</u>, and <u>Burden of Freedom</u>;

John Maxwell's <u>Developing the Leader Within You</u>, <u>The 360º Leader</u>, and <u>The 21 Irrefutable Laws of Leadership</u>; Rick Warren's <u>The Purpose Driven Life</u>; George C. Fraser's <u>CLICK</u>; and Larry Julian's <u>God is my CEO</u>. The good news is I found that most of my favorite books on leadership are **principle centered**, and **values based**. Also, a revelation hit me like morning light when curtains open in a dark room. The authors and writers all draw from the best book on leadership ever written and that is the **The Holy Bible.** The Bible is the dictionary of our scrabbled existence. All the answers to life's questions lie in its text and it is up to each of us to search and seek the meaning of its Word(s). As for leadership, where else can you find one man who started a company with twelve people and it continues to grow and pay dividends for over two thousand years? All other leaders dwarf in comparison to **Jesus Christ.**

> *"God alone is sovereign; His Way is perfert; His Word is flawless; and the final authority for my life."* Keith Osbourne

ABOUT THE AUTHOR

William "Bill" Minix, former military officer and Army Ranger, is the founder and president of StarWise, Inc., and MinixMarketing. Both companies share the vision of serving people by providing consulting, training, and access to products for personal and professional development. He utilizes over 25 years of professional experience, specializing in leadership development, consultative selling skills enhancement, and cultural change management. He lives by his company's motto, "We Grow Leaders, Who Grow Business." Bill is renowned for facilitating transformational learning experiences in self-awareness, self-management, performance development management, negotiations, communication, presentations, team building, and process change management. He holds an MBA from Lake Forest Graduate School of Management, and a Bachelor of Science in Education from Southern University. Bill created StarWise because he believes leadership development is the #1 area that individuals and organizations can enhance to improve performance. His methods have profoundly impacted major corporations, military personnel, academic leaders, and ordinary people seeking to grow their power and influence.

Ordering Information

For more information, to order other books and/or products, or to find out about bulk-order discounts please visit our website at www.getbestwebbusiness.com.

To book speaking engagements contact us at MinixMarketing@gmail.com or via our website at www.getbstwebbusiness.com.

Great Things Happen When Leaders Show Up!

www.ingramcontent.com/pod-product-compliance
Lightning Source LLC
Chambersburg PA
CBHW071429220526
45469CB00004B/1461